TRADING RULES FOR SUCCESS

The 9 Rules You Need to Know to Be Successful
and Ensure Continuous Income

Liam Elder

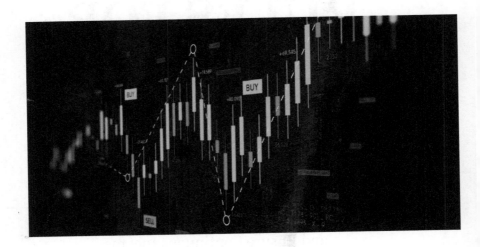

The information in the following pages is broadly considered
a truthful and accurate account of facts and as such, any
inattention, use, or misuse of the information in question by
the reader will render any resulting actions solely under their
purview. There are no scenarios in which the publisher or the

TABLE OF CONTENTS

INTRODUCTION 7

MANAGING YOUR DAY TRADES...9
ABCD PATTERN 11
BULL FLAG MOMENTUM...15

CHAPTER 1 APPLICATION ON THE COMMODITIES MARKET.........................18

WHAT IS FUNDAMENTAL ANALYSIS? 20
CLASSIFICATION OF COMMODITIES 22
INDIRECT INVESTMENTS IN COMMODITIES CAN BE MADE BY PLACING CAPITAL IN EQUITY. ..23

CHAPTER 2 APPLICATION ON THE CRYPTO VALUE MARKET 26

Ethereum...30
Crypto-Currency is Not Money 32

CHAPTER 3 APPLICATION ON THE STOCKS MARKET 34

CHAPTER 4 HOW DOES THE STOCK MARKET WORK? 46

STOCK MARKET CORRECTIONS AND CRASH 50
FUNDAMENTAL MARKET ANALYSIS 51
TECHNICAL MARKET ANALYSIS 53

CHAPTER 5 TOP DAY TRADING TOOLS 56

STOP LOSS MANAGEMENT 60
PENNY STOCK LEVEL 2 QUOTES...61

CHAPTER 6 MOMENTUM TRADING 64

CHAPTER 7 COMMON DAY TRADING MISTAKES TO AVOID..........................72

CHAPTER 8 PORTFOLIO DIVERSIFICATION..80

INTRODUCTION TO DIVERSIFICATION.....................................81
THE PROCESS OF ASSET CLASS ALLOCATION 85

CHAPTER 9 OPTIONS DAY TRADING RULES FOR SUCCESS..........................92

RULE FOR SUCCESS #1 – HAVE REALISTIC EXPECTATIONS 93
RULE FOR SUCCESS #2 – START SMALL TO GROW A BIG PORTFOLIO..........................94
RULE FOR SUCCESS #3 – KNOW YOUR LIMITS 94
RULE FOR SUCCESS #4 – BE MENTALLY, PHYSICALLY AND EMOTIONALLY PREPARED EVERY DAY 95
RULE FOR SUCCESS #5 – DO YOUR HOMEWORK DAILY...96
RULE FOR SUCCESS #6 – ANALYZE YOUR DAILY PERFORMANCE 97

RULE FOR SUCCESS #7 – DO NOT BE GREEDY...98

RULE FOR SUCCESS #8 – PAY ATTENTION TO VOLATILITY 98

RULE FOR SUCCESS #9 – USE THE GREEKS 99

CHAPTER 10 TRADING WITH THE TREND **100**

MARKET AWARENESS 102

SETTING PROFIT GOALS 105

DAY TRADING? 106

TRADING PUTS 107

CONCLUSION **108**

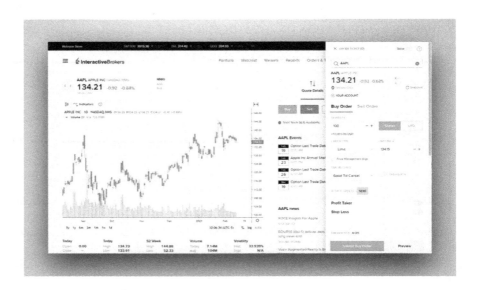

Introduction

It is essential that you understand and apply all these three elements in day trading. While some strategies only require technical indicators (like VWAP and Moving Average), it will help you a lot if you understand price action and chart patterns, so you can be a profitable day trader.

This knowledge, especially about price action comes only with regular practice. As a day trader, you must not care about the company and its revenue. You should not be distracted by the mission or vision of the company or how much money they make. Your focus must only be on the chart patterns, technical indicators, and price action.

Successful day traders also don't mix technical analysis with fundamental analysis. Day traders usually focus more on technical analysis.

The catalyst is the reason why a particular stock is running. If you have a stock that is running up to 70%, you need to determine the catalyst behind this change, and never stop until you figure that one out.

So, it's a tech company that just got patent approval or a pharmaceutical company that passed through important clinical trials. These are catalysts that can help you understand what is really going on.

Beyond this, don't bother yourself squinting over revenue papers or listening in conference calls. You should not care about these things unless you are a long-term investor.

Day traders trade fast. There are times that you may find yourself trading in time periods as short as 10 to 30 seconds, and can make thousands of dollars. If the market is moving fast, you need to make certain that you are in the right position to take advantage of the profits and minimize your risk exposure.

There are millions of day traders out there with different strategies. Each trader requires its strategy and edge. You must find your spot in the market whenever you feel comfortable.

You must focus on day trading strategies because these really work for day trading. The following strategies have been proven effective in day trading. These strategies are quite basic in theory, but they can be challenging to master and requires a lot of practice.

Also remember that in the market today, more than 60% of the volume is dominated by algorithmic trading. So you are really competing against computers. There's a big chance that you will lose against an algorithm. You may get lucky a couple of times, but supercomputers will win the game.

Trading stocks against computers means that the majority of the changes in stocks that you see are basically the result of computers moving shares around. On one hand, it also means that there are certain stocks every day that will be traded on such heavy retail volume.

Every day, you have to focus on trading these specific stocks or the Apex Predators - the stocks that are usually gapping down or up on revenue.

You should hunt for stocks that have considerable interest among day traders and considerable retail volume. These are the stocks that you can buy, and together, the retail traders can still win the game against algorithmic traders.

One principle in day trading that you may find useful is that you must only choose the setups that you want to master. Using basic trading methods that are composed of minimal setups is effective in reducing the stress and confusion, and will allow you to focus more on the psychological effect of trading. This will separate the losers from the winners.

Managing Your Day Trades

It is always intriguing when two-day traders choose the same stock - the one short and the other long.

More often than not, both traders become profitable, proving that trader management and experience are more important than the stock and the strategy used by the trader.

Remember, your trade size will depend on the price of the stock and your account and risk management. Beginners in day trading are recommended to limit the size of their shares below 1000.

For example, you can buy 800 shares, then sell half in the first target. You can bring your stop loss to break even. Then you can sell another 200 in the next target. You can keep the last 200 shares until you stop. You can always maintain some shares in case the price will keep on moving in your favor.

IMPORTANT: Professional day traders never risk their shares all at once.

They know how to scale into the trade, which means they buy shares at different points. They may start with 200 shares and then add to their position in different steps. For instance, for an 800-share trader, they could enter either 400/400 or 100/200/500 shares. When done properly, this is an excellent way to manage your trades and risks. But managing the position in the system can be overly difficult. Many newbies who may attempt to do this could end up over trading and may lose their money in slippage, commissions, and averaging down the losing stocks. Rare is the chance that you may scale into a trade. Still, there are times that you can do this, especially in high-volume trades.

However, you should take note that scaling into a trade increases your risk and beginners can use it improperly as a way to average down their losing positions. We have discussed this for the sake of information, and this is not recommended for beginners.

Even though they may appear the same, there's a big difference between averaging down a losing position and scaling into a trade. For newbies, averaging down a losing position can wipe out your account, especially with small accounts that are not strong enough for averaging down.

ABCD Pattern

The ABCD Pattern is the simplest pattern you can trade, and this is an ideal choice for amateur day traders. Even though this is pretty much basic and has been used by day traders for a long time, it still works quite effectively because many day traders are still using it.

This pattern has a self-fulfilling prophecy effect, so you just follow the trend.

The chart above shows an example of an ABCD pattern in the stock market. This one begins with a strong upwards move. Buyers are quickly buying stocks as represented by point A, and making new highs in point B. In this trend, you may choose to enter the trade, but you must not be overly obsessed with the trade, because, at point B, it can be quite extended and at its highest price.

Moreover, you can't ascertain the stop for this pattern. Take note that you should never enter a trade without identifying your stop. At point B, traders who purchased the stock earlier begin gradually selling it for profit and the prices will also come down.

Still, you must not enter the trade because you are not certain where the bottom of this trend will be. But if you see that the price doesn't come down from a specific level such as point C, it means that the stock has discovered possible support.

Thus, you can plan your trade and set up the stops and a point to take the profits.

For example, OPTT (Ocean Power Technologies Inc) announced in 2016 that they closed a new $50 million deal. This one is a good example of a fundamental catalyst. OPTT stocks surged from $7.70 (Point A) to $9.40 (B) at around 9 am. Day traders who were not aware of the news waited for point B and then an indication that the stock will not go lower than a specific price (C).

If you saw that C holds support and buyers are fighting back to allow the stock price to go any lower than the price at C, you will know that the price will be higher. Buyers jumped on massively.

Remember, the ABCD Pattern is a basic day trading strategy,

and many retail traders are looking for it. Near point D, the volume immediately spiked, which means that the traders are now in the trade. When the stock made a new low, it was a clear exit signal.

Here are the specific steps you can follow to use the ABCD strategy:

1. Whenever you see that a stock is surging up from point A and about to reach a new high for the day (point B), then wait to see if the price makes support higher than A. You can mark this as point C, but don't jump right into it.

2. Monitor the stock during its consolidation phase, then choose your share size and plan your stop and exit.

3. If you see that the price is holding support at point C, then you can participate in the trade closer to the price point C to anticipate the move to point D or even higher.

4. Your stop could be at C. When the price goes lower than C, you can sell. Thus, it is crucial to buy the stock closer to C to reduce the loss. (Some day traders have a higher tolerance, so they wait a bit more near D to ensure that the ABCD pattern is complete. However, this is risky as it can reduce your profit).

5. When the price moves higher, you can sell half of your shares near point D, and bring your stop higher to your breakeven point.

6. Sell the rest of your shares as soon as you hit your target or you feel that the price is losing momentum, or that the sellers are getting control of the price action.

Bull Flag Momentum

Expert stock analysts consider the Bull Flag Momentum as a scalping strategy because the flags in the pattern don't usually last long. Plus, day traders should scalp the trade to get in quickly, make money, and then exit the market.

Below is an example of a Bull Flag pattern with one notable consolidation.

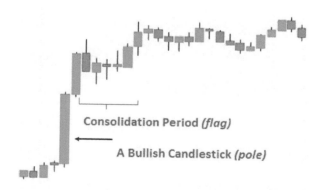

Consolidation Period *(flag)*

A Bullish Candlestick *(pole)*

This chart is called Bull Flag because it is like a flag on a pole. In this pattern, you have different large candles rising (pole) and you also have a sequence of small candles that move sideways (flag) or "consolidating" in day trading jargon.

When there is consolidation in the pattern, it signifies that traders who purchased the stocks at a lower price are now selling. While this is happening, the price doesn't significantly decrease because buyers are still participating in the trades, and sellers are not yet in control of the price. Many retail traders will miss buying the stock before the Bull Flag begins. Buying stocks when the price is increasing could be risky. This is known as "chasing the stock". Successful day traders usually aim to participate in the trade during quiet periods and take their profits during wild periods.

Chapter 1

Application on the Commodities Market

Trading in the commodity markets based on fundamental news and analysis differs dramatically from the quick-natured technical analysis, which often requires traders to shift from bullish to bearish in the blink of an eye. Fundamental analysis provides slow-handed guidance to traders. In general, the practice of entering or exiting trades based on market fundamentals is a dawdling and tedious process, demanding massively deep pockets and patience. Imagine being a fundamentalist who identified oil as being overvalued near $100 per barrel in 2008, or on multiple occasion's oil moved above $100 from 2011 to 2013.

Initially, a trader selling a futures contract solely on fundamentals would have either blown out his trading account, given up on the trade before it paid off, or suffered a roughly $50,000 drawdown before having an opportunity to profit from the correct analysis. This is because each dollar of crude oil price change equals a profit or loss of $1,000 to a one-lot futures trader. In 2008, the price of oil reached $150 per barrel before suffering from a steep decline. On subsequent occasions, the suffering would have been limited to about $10,000 to $15,000, but still a painful endeavor.

If you are familiar with the popular commodity trading book *Hot Commodities*, written by Jim Rogers, this slow-paced fundamental approach is exactly what he writes about. Not all of us have the capital to employ such a long-term view in the leveraged world of commodities, as Mr. Rogers does. Accordingly, before assuming commodity trading is as "easy" as that particular book implies, you must consider the vast financial difference in the reality of most commodity traders and the author.

Other than obtaining a big-picture consensus of the market makeup, relying on fundamental analysis alone can be a daunting task for the average trader. After all, it can take months, or even years, for traders to get their hands on absolutely accurate fundamental information. By then, the markets have already moved. Alternatively, during times in which markets are ignoring fundamentals, it can take months, or years, for prices to revert to a more equilibrium price.

What Is Fundamental Analysis?

Fundamental analysis of the commodity markets involves the study of the interaction between supply and demand; with this analysis, traders attempt to predict future price movements. Specifically, the entire concept of fundamental analysis is built upon the following equations:

Demand > Supply = Higher prices

Supply > Demand = Low prices

Most analysts agree that commodity market supply and demand figures are quantifiable, yet even the diehard fundamentalists will admit accurate statistics are not available in real-time. Thus, any numbers plugged into the simple and neat formulas given are relatively meaningless. If you input garbage data into the formula, the result will also be garbage. Accordingly, when an analyst runs the numbers she is almost certainly working with either outdated or inaccurate data. Fundamental analysts waiting for confirmed government supply and demand data will be calculating months after the fact. Alternatively, if they are calculating based on estimates (whether they are government or personally derived), it is nothing more than a guess.

Most recall the simple supply and demand cross charts taught in high school and college economic courses; unfortunately, this academic practice erroneously simplifies a concept that is actually, highly complex. In my opinion, what appears to be the most straightforward form of commodity market analysis—fundamental—is the most difficult in practice.

Because of the massive complexity that comes with estimating the current supply and demand details of any given commodity, the seemingly simple mathematical equation fundamentalists use to speculate on prices can be confusing at best but misleading at worst. Also, regardless of the time dedicated to deciphering the market's fundamental code, it can be extremely problematic for a trader to succeed using this method of analysis alone.

To understand the place of the commodity markets, one needs to consider the bigger picture.

Asset classes are certainly not limited to these five groups, but these are the most common categories. Any classification is rather arbitrary or, at least, subjective. Even wine or art can be seen as specific asset classes, as much as volatility or weather. Based on any assets, including the latter, derivatives or structured products can be developed and traded.

Classification of commodities

Zooming in on the asset class commodities could lead to identifying subcategories. At the further detailed level, more subclasses can be identified. Metals can be split into precious and non-precious metals. Indirect investments Nowadays, the ownership of shares, bonds, or currencies is registered digitally. Consequently, the transfer of title takes place without physical hassle. The physical process, however, is unavoidable with commodities. As they are consumed physically they also have to be transported materially. Analogously, the storage of commodities requires physical storage capacity. Nevertheless, investors and financial traders who would like to be exposed to commodity prices typically dislike purchasing commodities physically, because then they must store the actual products. However, most of these market participants do not hold tangible storage capacity. Moreover, most of them do not want to be involved with the relevant concrete matters at all. This is why investments are made indirectly. Luckily for them, exposures can be created in many ways.

Indirect investments in commodities can be made by placing capital in equity.

One could, for instance, buy shares of mining firms, oil and gas companies, or corporates which produce or process agricultural products. However, this brings risk beyond commodity prices. After all, a stock price is not just influenced by the relevant commodity price. Moreover, a corporate share price is impacted by numerous drivers, amongst which are the management, logistical success or failures, and operational performance, but also the management and possibly even accounting scandals. This often leads to a discrepancy between the stock price development and the underlying commodity price development. This basis risk could work two ways, namely in favor or adversely. One could profit from leverage but, on the other side, one may want to avoid underperformance. Therefore, investors often seek an alternative indirect investment opportunity, with a more direct relationship. Commodity derivatives provide such an alternative. A commodity derivatives contract is an agreement whereby the underlying value typically concerns a commodity or commodity index. Examples of commodity derivatives are commodity futures, commodity options, and commodity swaps.

Commodity markets are complex systems

Before taking a position in commodities, an investor or market participant has to realize that the commodity markets are much more complex than capital markets, FX markets, or money markets. After all, commodity markets face most elements that drive and influence typical financial markets, but on top of that, commodity markets are severely impacted by many more driving forces, such as politics, weather circumstances, and the availability plus utilization of production, consumption, transport and storage capacity. For this reason, one requires in-depth knowledge about technical aspects. A background in engineering or physics would be quite helpful to understand the commodity supply chains and, hence, the commodity markets. Compared to the money markets, commodity markets are relatively new, and thus far from mature. Also, they face relatively many fundamental price driving factors, they are significantly impacted by economic cycles and they are typically exposed to a relatively large number of events. As a consequence of the later, commodity prices face relatively high volatility, especially in the spot markets. Moreover, some commodity markets can even show negative prices. In addition, commodity markets, compared to money markets, are characterized by a relatively weak relationship between spot and forward prices, have to

Deal with strong seasonality, show fragmented markets instead of centralization, and face relatively complex derivatives.

Chapter 2

Application on the Crypto Value Market

The queries whether crypto-currencies follow structured chart behaviors similar to the normal economic markets has been presented by several traders. Admittedly, crypto-currencies similar to Bitcoin and Ethereum act very well owing to the dearth of elementary players whose supposition can be opposite to the actual behavior of crypto-currency prices. These charts are unpredictable when it comes to the fluctuation of price but can be effective as far as the prediction of the potential behavior of price is concerned.

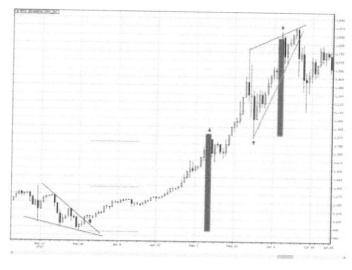

The effective representation of basic graphical patterns across this period is evident from the left to right side of the graph.

The upper points on the graph show the breakout of a falling wedge to determine the initial point of the wedge.

The breakout of the consolidation zone is directed upwards. The target is labeled thus stopping the move.

The upper target estimated by the block keeps the trend moving upwards leading to fulfillment and the beginning of a stronger pullback.

The breakout of the rising wedge is directed towards the downside. The results are indicated in the next chart.

The breakout of the rising wedge is followed by the pullback from an extended move.

A measured move target that is ready is likely to bring about the multi-down leg.

The measured move target can also be achieved by the tagged wedge break target. This eliminates the need to go low.

As the falling wedge is considered the unusual pattern of topping, there was an expectation of a year-high test.

The step by step explanation is given to facilitate your understanding.

The fundamental graphical pattern will represent the reasonable forecasting power on near-term price movements, as long as a standardized market exists for the trading of any instrument. In other words, if the trader is only focused on his profits, the graph pattern will depict the expected outcomes of market behavior. Since different types of people are engaged in crypto-currency trade and financial markets, it's obvious that the fluctuation of the price will also be different for both types of trades.

Due to the introduction of futures contracts on Bitcoin, however, this situation is changing. This enables the experienced trade firm employees to trade crypto-currencies under the protective regulations offered by various exchanges such as the Chicago Board of Trade and the Chicago Mercantile Exchange. It is expected that the huge financial organizations will shortly take over the current crypto-currency players.

To sum it up, Bitcoin is expected to act similarly to a developing regulated derivatives market. Due to the possible use of arbitrage algorithms for trading Bitcoin with financial institutes, greater correspondence is seen

between the price actions of the bitcoin and other financial markets. Contrary to the claims of bitcoin promoters, bitcoin is now becoming the financial tool intended to serve a particular purpose.

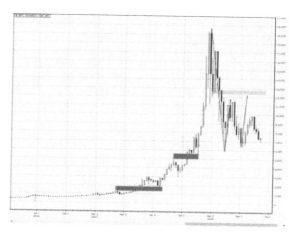

The next move of the bitcoin is still the main query forwarded by many after it deviated from the ever-high of 19666. It must amaze many that the stock market bottom with S&P 500 is printing a low of 666. The main thing here is not if there is any conspiracy involved behind this and we will only focus on the facts depicted from charts.

The chart shown above shows the Bitcoin details.

In the year 2017, a couple of pockets were left behind by the massive upwards movement towards the blow-off. It was expected that the higher one will be tagged; however, it did not occur till now. This implies that Bitcoin is still expected to trade between 5500 and 5600 before trading over 12600 which was its level at 2017 closing.

The movement of the bitcoin to the 2017 closure of 12600 from the existing level of trading over 7000 (May 2018) will be considered as the complex multiple leg move. This movement is expected to be followed with immediate selling most probably targeting the low pockets.

Considering the time taken by the bitcoin to move above 19000, it is logical to expect the bitcoin to require a similar time period to grasp this move.

It is appropriate to check the bottoming of the bitcoin as long as there is no formation of a weekly level bottom pattern. Although it may require a lot of patience by Perma bulls to wait for the bottoming of bitcoin, it is worth waiting since it may fell down boundlessly.

Ethereum

The peak of the bitcoin was followed by the peak of various other crypto-currencies particularly Ethereum which showed a rise to maximum position in January 2018. This may be attributed to the hype created by Bitcoin at that time. More interesting is the fact that Ethereum doubled even after the fall of bitcoin. Such a movement was new for Ethereum however; bitcoin has seen this up and down many times.

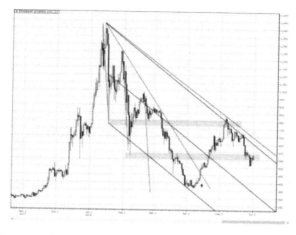

Three downside pushes are evident from Ethereum's pullback structure. The Ethereum put an end to this move before reaching the third downside target. This was done through the resistance trend line's breakout shown by an upward arrow.

The breakout leads to an upward move towards the peak of the channel due to the swing lows developed in the pullback process.

It resulted in a situation where the second swing held more importance. Currently, Ethereum is being traded at this zone (as at end of May 2018). In case of maintenance of this level, we can expect an upward move towards the start of the pullback as per the indication of the three pushes down pattern. The highest-ever level of Ethereum is the start of pullback. The potential situation of bitcoin is different from this situation of Ethereum.

However, this is not that simple. The daily charts still reveal a downtrend with a strong resistance being shown by the down channel top. Ethereum will not move upwards and will be kept low as long as the channel top is not cleared. The channel top will cause Ethereum to break the record of the lowest level made in May 2018. Keeping the channel midpoint as the main target, even lower prices are expected. Currently (as of the end of May 2018), the mid-channel level is almost 300.

Crypto-Currency is Not Money

In my opinion, I must clarify the fact that crypto-currencies would not be able to rule the world in their current position as claimed by their promoters. They are not a valuable source or a monetary form. Although the concept of the significance of the crypto-currency for restoring trust was reasonable, it could not yield the desired results because of technological issues and issues in practical execution. However, no significant harm was caused to the assets.

The longing to make money from technological advancements led to the emergence of various ideas. In particular, the advent of crypto-currencies is expected to bring revolutions in future transactions. It is expected that the crypto-currency concept will bring about technological advancements causing massive revolutions in all aspects.

It is not easy to determine the crypto-currency that can

endure the current bearish market trends. Even if one determines the right kind of crypto-currency, it is expected to lose its significance with the technological advancements in the similar manner in which the advent of Facebook rendered the previous social media platforms obsolete.

Trading in crypto-currencies must involve a lot of caution on part of the trader since it is a hazardous play. It is better to understand the risky nature of crypto-currencies so that you don't put the amount you cannot afford to lose for betting. This statement is right for all types of trades. There is no emphasis on the management of risk to be the only factor of concern for the survival of a trader in this market.

Chapter 3

Application on the Stocks Market

Astock is a form of security that suggests proportional ownership in a company. Stocks are acquired and sold predominantly on stock exchanges, however, there can be private arrangements as well. These exchanges/trades need to fit within government laws which are expected to shield investors from misleading practices. Stocks can be obtained from a large number of online platforms.

Businesses issue (offer) stock to raise capital. The holder of stock (a shareholder) has now acquired a portion of the company and shares its profit and loss. Therefore, a a shareholder is considered an owner of the company.

Ownership is constrained by the number of shares an individual owns regarding the number of shares the company is divided into. For example, if a company has 1,000 shares of stock and one individual owns 100 shares, that individual would receive 10% of the company's capital and profits.

Financial experts don't own companies as such; instead, they sell shares offered by companies. Under the law, there are different types of companies and some are viewed as independent because of how they have set up their businesses. Regardless of the type of company, ultimately, they must report costs, income, changes in structure, etc., or they can be sued. A business set up as an "independent," known as a sole proprietorship, suggests that the owner assumes all responsibilities and is liable for all financial aspects of the business. A business set up as a company of any sort means that the business is separate from its owners and the owners aren't personally responsible for the financial aspects of the business.

This separation is of extreme importance; it limits the commitment of both the company and the shareholder/owner. If the business comes up short, a judge may rule for the company to be liquidated – however, your very own assets will not come under threat. The court can't demand that you sell your shares, though the value of your shares will have fallen significantly.

Trading is the basic idea of exchanging one thing for another. In this regard, it is buying or selling, where compensation is paid by a buyer to a seller. Trade can happen inside an economy among sellers and buyers. Overall, trade allows countries to develop markets for the exchange of goods and services that for the most part wouldn't have been available otherwise. It is the reason why an American purchaser can choose between a Japanese, German, or American conduit. Due to overall trade, the market contains progressively significant competition which makes it possible for buyers to get products and services at affordable costs.

In fiscal markets, trading implies the buying and selling of insurances, for instance, the purchase of stock on the New York Stock Exchange (NYSE).

Fundamentals of stock/securities exchange

The exchange of stocks and securities happens on platforms like the New York Stock Exchange and Nasdaq. Stocks are recorded on a specific exchange, which links buyers and sellers, allowing them to trade those stocks. The trade is tracked in the market and allows buyers to get company stocks at fair prices. The value of these stocks moves – up or down – depending on many factors in the market. Investors can look at these factors and decide on whether or not they want to purchase these stocks.

A market record tracks the value of a stock, which either addresses the market with everything considered or a specific fragment of the market. You're likely going to hear most about the S&P 500, the Nasdaq composite, and the Dow Jones Industrial Average in this regard.

Financial advisors use data to benchmark the value of their portfolios and, some of the time, to shed light on their stock exchanging decisions. You can also put your assets into an entire portfolio based on the data available in the market.

Stock exchanging information

Most financial experts would be well-taught to build a portfolio with a variety of different financial assets. However, experts who prefer a greater degree of movement take more interest in the stock exchange. This type of investment incorporates the buying and selling of stocks.

The goal of people who trade in stock is to use market data and things happening in the market to either sell the stock for a profit or buy stocks at low prices to make a profit later. Some stock traders are occasional investors, which means they buy and sell now and then. Others are serious investors, making as little as twelve exchanges for every month.

Financial experts who exchange stocks do wide research, as often as possible, devoting hours day by day tracking the market. They rely upon particular audits, using instruments to chart a stock's advancements attempting to find trading openings and examples. Various online middlemen offer stock exchanging information, including expert reports, stock research, and charting tools.

What is a bear market?

A bear market means stock prices are falling — limits move to 20% or more — based on data referenced previously.

Progressive financial experts may be alright with the term bear market. Profiting in the trade business will always far outlast the typical bear market; which is why in a bear market, smart investors will hold their shares until the market recovers. This has been seen time and time again. The S&P 500, which holds around 500 of the greatest stocks in the U.S., has consistently maintained an average of around 7% consistently when you factor in reinvested profits and varied growth. That suggests that if you invested $1,000 30 years ago, you could have around $7,600 today.

Stock market crash versus a correction

A crash happens when the commercial value prices fall by 10% or more. It is an unexpected, incredibly sharp fall in stock prices; for example, in October 1987, when stocks dove 23%

in a single day.

The stock market tends to be affected longer by crashes in the market and can last from two to nine years.

The criticalness of improvement

You can't avoid the possibility of bear markets or the economy crashing, or even losing money while trading. What you can do, however, is limit the effects these types of the market will have on your investment by maintaining a diversified portfolio.

Diversification shields your portfolio from unavoidable market risks. If you dump a large portion of your cash into one means of investment, you're betting on growth that can rapidly turn to loss by a large number of factors.

To cushion risks, financial specialists expand by pooling different types of stocks together, offsetting the inevitable possibility that one stock will crash and your entire portfolio will be affected or you lose everything.

You can put together individual stocks and assets in a single portfolio. One recommendation: dedicate 10% or less of your portfolio to a few stocks you believe in each time you decide to invest.

Ways to invest

There are different ways for new investors to purchase stocks. If you need to pay very low fees, you will need to invest additional time making your own trades. If you wish to beat the market, however, you'll pay higher charges by getting someone to trade on your behalf. If you don't have the time or interest, you may need to make do with lower results.

Most stock purchasers get anxious when the market is doing well. Incredibly, this makes them purchase stocks when they are the most volatile. Obviously, business share that is not performing well triggers fear. That makes most investors sell when the costs are low.

Choosing what amount to invest is an individual decision. It depends upon your comfort with risk. It depends upon your ability and capacity to invest energy into getting some answers concerning the stock exchange.

Purchase Stocks Online

Purchasing stocks online costs, the least, yet gives little encouragement. You are charged a set price, or a percent of your purchase, for every trade. It very well may be the least secure. It expects you to teach yourself altogether on the best way to invest. Consequently, it additionally takes the most time. It's a smart idea to check the top web-based trading sites before you begin.

Investment Groups

Joining an investment group gives you more data at a sensible price. However, it takes a great deal of effort to meet with the other group members. They all have different degrees of expertise. You might be required to pool a portion of your assets into a group account before trading. Once more, it's a smart idea to examine the better investment groups before you begin.

Full-time Brokers

A full-time broker is costly because you'll pay higher fees. Nevertheless, you get more data and assistance and that shields you from greed and fear. You should search around to choose a decent broker that you can trust. The Securities and Trade Commission shares helpful tips on the best ways to choose a broker.

Money Manager

Money managers select and purchase the stocks for you. You pay them a weighty charge, typically 1-2 percent of your complete portfolio. If the chief progresses admirably, it takes a minimal amount of time. That is because you can simply meet with them more than once per year. Ensure you realize how to choose a decent financial advisor.

File Fund

Otherwise called market traded assets, record assets can be a cheap and safe approach to benefit from stocks. They essentially track the stocks in a file. Models incorporate the MSCI developing business sector record. The reserve rises and falls alongside the file. There is no yearly cost. However, it's difficult to outflank the market along these lines since record supports just track the market. All things being equal, there is a great deal of valid justifications for why you ought to put resources into a file fund.

Common Funds

Common assets are a generally more secure approach to benefit from stocks. The company supervisor will purchase a gathering of stocks for you. You don't possess the stock, yet a portion of the investment. Most assets have a yearly cost, between 0.5 percent to 3 percent. They guarantee to outflank the S&P 500, or other equivalent file reserves. For additional information, see 16 Best Tips on Mutual Fund Basics and Before You Buy a Mutual Fund.

Theories of stock investments

Theories of stock investments look like basic resources. Both of them pool all of their investors' dollars into one viably supervised hold. In any case, theories stock investments put assets into ensnared fiscal instruments known as subordinates. They guarantee to win the normal resources with these significantly used theories.

Theoretical stock investments are private companies, not open organizations. That suggests they aren't coordinated by the SEC. They are risky, yet various investors acknowledge this higher danger prompts a better yield.

Selling Your Stocks

As important as buying stocks is knowing when to sell them. Most financial experts buy when the stock exchange is rising and sell when it's falling. Regardless, a clever money marketer seeks after a strategy subject to their financial needs.

You should reliably watch out for the noteworthy market records. The three greatest U.S. records are the Dow Jones Industrial Average, the S&P 500, and the Nasdaq. In any case, don't solidify in case they enter a modification or a mishap. Those events don't prop up long.

Chapter 4

How Does The Stock Market Work?

The stock market is not like your neighborhood grocery store: you can only buy and sell through licensed brokers who make trades on major indexes like NASDAQ and S&P 100. This is where investors meet up to buy and sell stocks or other financial investments like bonds. The stock market is made up of so many exchanges, like the NASDAQ or the New York Exchange. These exchanges are not open all through the day. Most exchanges like the NASDAQ and NYSE are open from 9:30 am to 4 pm. EST. Although premarket and trading after closing time now exist, not all brokers do this.

Companies list their stocks on an exchange in a bid to raise money for their business, and investors buy those shares. In addition to this, investors can trade shares among themselves, and the exchange keeps track of the rate of supply and demand of each listed stock. The rate of supply and demand for stocks determines the price. If there's a high demand for a particular stock, its price tends to rise. On the other hand, the price of a stock goes down when there's less demand for it. The stock market computer algorithm handles these varying fluctuations in prices.

How Does The Stock Market Work?

A Stock market analysis definitely looks like gibberish to beginners and average investors. However, you should know that the way this market works is actually quite simple. Just imagine a typical auction house or an online auction website. This market works in the same way - it allows buyers and sellers to negotiate prices and carry out successful trades. The first stock market took place in a physical marketplace, however, these days, trades happen electronically via the internet and online stockbrokers. From the comfort of your homes, you can easily bid and negotiate for the prices of stocks with online stockbrokers.

Furthermore, you might come across news headlines that say the stock market has crashed or gone up. Once again, don't fret or get all excited when you come across such news. Most often than not, this means a stock market index has gone up or down. In other words, the stocks in a market index have gone down. Before we proceed, let's explore the meaning of market indexes.

Stock Market Indexes

Market indexes track the performance of a group of stocks in a particular sector like manufacturing or technology. The value of the stocks featured in an index is representative of all the stocks in that sector. It is very important to take note of what stocks each market index represents. In addition to this, giant market indexes like the Dow Jones Industrial Average, the NASDAQ composite, and the Standard & Poor's 500, are often used as proxies for the performance of the stock market as a whole. You can choose to invest in an entire index through the exchange-traded funds and index funds, as it can track a specific sector or index of the stock market.

Bullish and Bearish Markets

Talking about the bullish outlook of the stock market is guaranteed to get beginners looking astonished. Yes, it sounds ridiculous at first, but with time, you get to appreciate the ingenuity of these descriptions. Let's start with the bearish market. A bear is an animal you would never want to meet on a hike; it strikes fear into your heart, and that's the effect you will get from a bearish market. The threshold for a bearish market varies within a 20 percent loss or more.

Most young investors unfamiliar with a bear market as we've been in a bull market since the first quarter of 2019. In fact, this makes it the second-longest bull market in history. Just as you have probably guessed by now, a bull market indicates that stock prices are rising. You should know that the market is continually changing from bull to bear and vice versa. From the Great Recession to the global market crash, these changing market prices indicate the start of larger economic patterns. For instance, a bull market shows that investors are investing heavily and that the economy is doing extremely well. On the other hand, a bear market shows investors are scared and pulling back, with the economy on the brink of collapsing. If this made you paranoid about the next bear market, don't fret. Business analysts have shown that the average bull market generally outlasts the average bear market by a large margin. This is why you can grow your money in stocks over an extended period of time.

Stock Market Corrections and Crash

A stock market crash is every investor's nightmare. It is usually extremely difficult to watch stocks that you've spent so many years accumulating diminish before your very eyes. Yes, this is how volatile the stock market is. Stock market crashes usually include a very sudden and sharp drop in stock prices, and it might herald the beginning of a bear market. On the other hand, stock market corrections occur when the market drops by 10 percent - this is just the market's way of balancing itself. The current bull market has gone through 5 market corrections.

Analyzing the Stock Market

You are not psychic. It is nearly impossible to accurately predict the outcome of your stock to the last detail. However, you can become near perfect at reading the stock market by learning how to properly analyze the components of this market. There are two basic types of analyses: technical analysis and fundamental analysis.

Fundamental Market Analysis

Fundamental analysis involves getting data about a company's stocks or a particular sector in the stock market, via financial records, company assets, economic reports, and market share. Analysts and investors can conduct fundamental analysis via the metrics on a corporation's financial statement. These metrics include cash flow statements, balance sheet statements, footnotes, and income statements. Most times, you can get a company's financial statement through a 10-k report in the database. In addition to this, the SEC's EDGAR is a good place to get the financial statement of the company you are interested in. With the financial statement, you can deduce the revenues, expenses, and profits a company has made.

What's more? By looking at the financial statement, you will have a measure of a company's growth trajectory, leverage, liquidity, and solvency. Analysts utilize different ratios to make an accurate prediction about stocks. For example, the quick ratio and current ratio are useful in determining if a company will be able to pay its short-term liabilities with the current asset. If the current ratio is less than 1, the company is in poor financial health and may not be able to recover from its short-term debt. Here's another example: a stock analyst can use the debt ratio to measure the current level of debt taken on by the company. If the debt ratio is above 1, it means the company has more debt than assets and it's only a matter of time before it goes under.

Technical Market Analysis

This is the second part of stock market analysis and it revolves around studying past market actions to predict the stock price direction. Technical analysts put more focus on the price and volume of shares. Additionally, they analyze the market as a whole and study the supply and demand factors that dictate market movement. In technical analyses, charts are of inestimable value. Charts are a vital tool as they show the graphical representation of a stock's trend within a set time frame. What's more? Technical investors are able to identify and mark certain areas as resistance or support levels on a chart. The resistance level is a previous high stock price before the current price. On the other hand, support levels are represented by a previous low before the current stock price. Therefore, a break below the support levels marks the beginning of a bearish trend. Alternatively, a break above the resistance level marks the beginning of a bullish market trend. Technical analysis is only effective when the rise and fall of stock prices are influenced by supply and demand forces. However, technical analysis is mostly rendered ineffective in the face of outside forces that affect stock prices such as stock splits, dividend announcements, scandals, changes in management, mergers, and so on. Investors can make use of both types of analyses to get an accurate prediction of their stock values.

Why You Need To Diversify

According to research by Ned Davis, a bear market occurs every 3.5 years and has an average lifespan of 15 months. One thing is clear, though: you can't avoid bear markets. You can, however, avoid the risks that come with investing in a single investment portfolio. Let's look at a common mistake that new investors typically make. Research points to the fact that individual stocks dwindle to a loss of 100 percent. By throwing in your lot with one company, you are exposing yourself to many setbacks. For example, you can lose your money if a corporation is embroiled in a scandal, poor leadership, and regulatory issues. So, how can you balance out your losses? By investing in a therefore mentioned index fund or ETF fund, as these indexes hold many different stocks, as by doing this, you've automatically diversified your investment. Here's a nugget to cherish: put 90 percent of your investment funds in an index fund, and put the remaining 10 percent in an individual stock that you trust.

When to Sell Your Stocks

One thing is sure - you are not going to hold your stocks forever. All our investment advice and energies are directed towards buying. Yes, it is the buying of stocks that kick-start the whole investment when chasing your dream concept. However, just as every beginning has an end, you will eventually sell every stock you buy. It is the natural order. Even so, selling off stock is not an easy decision. Heck! It's even harder to determine the right time to sell. This is the point where greed and human emotions start to battle with pragmatism. Many investors try to make sensible selling decisions solely based on price movements. However, this is not a sure strategy, as it is still sensible to hold onto a stock that has fallen in value. Conversely, selling a stock when it has reached your target is seen as prudent. So, how can you navigate around this dilemma?

Chapter 5

Top Day Trading Tools

Software Tools

Retail traders, in particular, can already access almost the same kinds of programs used by institutional traders. Moreover, many of these tools are either available online or downloadable on the computer. In fact, with the growing popularity of mobile devices such as tablets and smartphones, some of these programs can also be downloaded on these devices. This way, you can trade anytime and anywhere even when you're on a holiday or commuting. These software tools can include:

Stock Screeners

A stock screener is a tool that allows you to compare company stocks against a set of criteria, which can include share price, market capitalization, dividend yield, volatility, valuation ratios, and analyst estimates.

What I like about stock screeners is they are very easy to use since the parameters can already be provided for you. All you have to do is to choose.

Now I can get more information on every company or narrow my search some more so I have fewer but hopefully, better-choice stocks to consider.

Stock screeners can be an excellent tool too to begin your research. It guides you on what kind of information to look for as you can see in the MORE INFO column. You can save more time as well. Note, though, that not all stock screeners have the same features. Some are pretty basic while others are comprehensive they can also let you run screening for other types of securities like bonds and mutual funds, like Yahoo Finance.

Auto Traders

Also known as automatic trading systems, these are programs that execute buys and sells on your behalf. Normally, you just set certain parameters, and they do the rest. One of the biggest advantages of auto trading is you don't have to constantly keep track of your trading literally as the system does it for you. In fact, over the years, it has become more sophisticated that it can already "read" historical data and provide you with recommendations or information so you can make more correct decisions. Also, you can execute the same commands multiple times on any given day and trade several accounts or orders at any given time.

However, there are downsides. First, there's disruption of the markets. In 2014 over 70% of trading is due to these automated systems. Now imagine if every trader executes huge orders every single time. Market movements can then become incredibly erratic. Moreover, even if these systems are designed to work more powerfully than any trader's thinking and analytical capacity, they are still prone to glitches, and these glitches can be disastrous. For example, it can place large orders that you don't want to in the first place.

Streaming Quotes

You can also consider this as your equivalent to a ticker tape. The only difference is that you'll get more information from streaming quotes.

Now streaming quotes are quotes displayed in real-time, so don't be surprised if the numbers tend to change very fast for certain stocks. It only goes to show that the market is active. For a day trader, streaming quotes are a valuable tool as they can help you make decisions including corrections on the fly. You can spot emerging buying and selling trends and analyze real-time charts. NASDAQ has an example of a streaming quote, although it's much simpler than the others like Quotestream or Scottrader.

Live Market Analysis

Although technical analysis is essential in day trading, you should also not neglect fundamental analysis as the latter can even dictate the results of the former. For this reason, I also use Live Market Analysis.

Live Market Analysis is simply a collection of any information, news, press releases, and reports pertaining to the companies that are being traded. They may not be directly related to finance (e.g., news about mergers or acquisitions) but they can influence stock price movement within the day.

You can source the analysis online such as Yahoo or Google Finance.

Stop Loss Management

I hope I've already established the fact that stop loss is incredibly important as part of your risk management strategy.

Learning Markets gives us two more options. These are the support and moving average methods.

Support levels refer to the level in which stock price dips the lowest before it goes high up. When you look at a fall below the uptrend is the support level. In the support method, your stop loss can be placed just a bit below the previous support level as this assumes that going below the stop-loss price means a continuous or longer downtrend for the stock.

Investopedia, on the other hand, has a good definition of moving averages. One of the benefits of this is that it cancels out "noise" or fluctuations that may not be that consistent. In other words, it gives you a clear picture of the possible movement of stock prices. For the stop loss setup, you can determine the moving average and have it just below the moving average.

Penny Stock Level 2 Quotes

Once in a while, day traders look for a penny stock, although the name can be a misnomer since, according to the Securities and Exchange Commission (SEC), these stocks are those that have less than $5 per share value.

Some traders like penny stocks because there's a lot of room for appreciation, which means opportunities for a massive return. Moreover, a person's capital can go a long way with penny stocks. For example, if a person has $5,000, he can allocate $1,000 for penny stocks worth $3 each. This means he gets 300 shares (rounded off to the nearest hundreds). Compare that if he uses the same amount to buy shares worth $5.

However, there are several downsides to penny stocks. One, they are hard to come by and they are thinly traded. Therefore, there's not much technical information you can use to make good decisions about them. Second, they are usually not found

in major exchanges because they have failed to meet some of the requirements or criteria. You may also have issues with liquidity, which means you may not be able to sell the stock quickly simply because penny stocks themselves are not that liquid.

Nevertheless, if you want to give penny stocks a try, you can use Level 2 Quotes, which is higher than the level 1 quote, which includes the streaming quote. An important data available in the level 2 quote is that of the market maker or those who have significant control of the market, including the brokerage firms. They are the ones who have massive volumes of order sizes, which they are going to trade. Market makers are meant to earn a profit, so orders may be holding off until they know they can make a gain. Traders in level 1, however, wouldn't know that. In level 2 quotes, traders can observe the movements of money makers and see what stocks they have the most interest in.

Chapter 6

Momentum Trading

Momentum is at the heart of all-day trading as finding trades with the right amount of momentum is the only way you can reliably guarantee a profit on your trades. Luckily, it is not unrealistic to expect to find at least one underlying asset that is likely to move as much as 30 percent each day due to the fact that all underlying assets with this much momentum all tend to share a few common technical indicators.

Momentum stock anatomy

While it might seem difficult to understand how anyone could expect to pick a stock with the right momentum out of the thousands of possible choices, the fact of the matter is that all high momentum stocks typically have several things in common. If you were given a list of 5,000 stocks, using the factors below you could likely come up with a list of 10 or less.

Float: The first thing you are going to want to keep in mind is that the stocks with the highest momentum are generally going to have a float that is less than 100 million shares. Float refers to the total number of shares that are currently available and can be found by taking the total number of outstanding shares and subtracting out all those that are restricted or are, functionally speaking, no longer traded. Restricted shares are those that are currently in the midst of a lockup period or other, similar restriction. The less float a stock has, the more volatility it is going to contain. Stocks with smaller float tend to have low liquidity and a higher bid/ask spread.

Daily charts: The next thing you are going to want to look for is stocks that are consistently beating their moving average and trending away from either the support or resistance depending on if you following a positive or negative trend.

Relative volume: You are also going to want to ensure that the stocks you are considering have a high amount of relative volume, with the minimum being twice what the current average is. The average you should consider in this case would be the current volume compared to the historical average for the stock in question. The standard volume is going to reset every night at midnight which means this is a great indicator when it comes to stocks that are seeing a higher than average amount of action right now.

Catalyst: While not, strictly speaking, required, you may still find it helpful to look for stocks that are currently having their momentum boosted by external sources. This can include things like activist investors, FDA announcements, and PR campaigns, and earnings reports.

Exit indicators to watch

Besides knowing what a potentially profitable momentum trade looks like, you are also going to need to know what to look for to ensure that you can successfully get while the getting is good. Keep the following in mind and you will always be able to get out without having to sacrifice any of your hard-earned profits.

Don't get greedy: It is important to set profit targets before you go into any trade, and then follow through on them when the trade turns in your favor. If you find yourself riding a stronger trend than you initially anticipated, the best choice is to instead sell off half of your holdings before setting a new and improved price target for the rest, allowing you to have your cake and eat it too.

Red candles: If you are not quite at your price target and you come across a candle that closes in the red then this is a strong the indicator that you should take what you have and exit ASAP.

If you have already sold off half of your holdings at this point, however, then you are going to want to go ahead and hold through the first red candle as long as it doesn't go so far as to actively trigger your stop loss.

Extension bar: An extension bar is a candle with a spike that causes dramatically increased profits. If this occurs you want to lock in your profits as quickly as possible as it is unlikely to last very long. This is your lucky day and it is important to capitalize on it.

Choosing a screener

Another important aspect of using a momentum strategy correctly is using a quality stock screen to find stocks that are trending towards the extreme ends of the market based on the criteria outlined above. A good screener is a virtually indispensable tool when it comes to narrowing down the field of potential options on any given day, the best of the best even lets you generate your unique filters that display a list of stocks that meet a variety of different criteria. What follows is a list of some of the most popular screeners on the market today.

StockFetchter: StockFetcher is one of the more complicated screeners out there, but all that complexity comes with a degree of power that is difficult to beat. Its power comes from a virtually unlimited number of parameters that its users can add to filter, ensuring that you only see exactly the types of stocks you are looking for. It offers a free as well as a paid version, the free version allows you to see the top five stocks that match your parameters while the paid version, $8.95 per month, shows you unlimited results.

Finviz: This site offers a wide variety of different premade filters that are designed to return results on the most promising stocks for a given day. It is extremely user-friendly as well and functions from three drop-down menus based on the type of indicator, technical, fundamental, or descriptive, and lets you choose the criteria for each. The results can then be sorted in a myriad of different ways to make it as easy to find the types of stocks you are looking for as possible. The biggest downside to Finviz is that it uses delayed data which means it is going to be most effective for those who run evening screens so they are ready to go when the market opens.

Chartmill: This site allows users to filter stocks based on many predetermined criteria including things like price, performance, volume, technical indicators, and candlestick patterns. It also offers up several more specialized indicators including things like squeeze plays, intensity, trend, and pocket pivots. This site works based on a credit system,

and every user is given 6,000 credits each month for free.

Every scan costs a few hundred credits so you should be able to take advantage of a variety of their tools virtually free of charge. Additional credits then cost $10 per 10,000 or they have an unlimited option available for about $30 per month.

Stockrover^l: This tool is specifically designed to cater to the Canadian market in addition to the US stock market. It offers up a variety of fundamental filters in addition to technical and performance-based options. This tool also allows you to track stocks that are near their established lows and high, those that may be gaining momentum, and even those that are seeing a lot of love from various hedge funds. Users also can create custom screens as well as unique equations for even more advanced screening. Users can also backtest their ideas to make sure that everything is working as intended. While their basic options are free to use, the more complex choices are gated behind a paywall that costs $250 for a year's subscription.

Know your filters

Day trading is about more than finding stocks that are high in volume, it is also about finding those that are currently experiencing a higher than average degree of movement as well. The following filters will help ensure that the stocks you find have plenty of both.

Steady volatility: To trade stocks that are extremely

volatile with as little research as possible, the following criterion is a good place to start. While additional research is always going to be preferable in the long run, you can find success if you run this scan once a week and pay close attention to the results.

This list should ideally return stocks that have moved at least 5 percent every day for the past 50 days. It is important to use a minimum of 50 days, though 75 or 100 will produce even more reliable results overall. Results of this magnitude will show that the stock in question has moved a significant amount over the past few months which means it is likely to continue to do so for the near future. The second criterion will determine the amount you should be willing to pay per share and can be altered based on your personal preferences.

The third criterion will determine the level of volume that you find acceptable for the given timeframe. The example will look for volume that is greater than four million shares within the past month. From there, it will eliminate leverage ETFs from the results which can be eliminated if you are interested in trading ETFs. Finally, the add column will show the list of stocks with the largest amount of volume and the greatest overall amount of movement. Selecting these columns will then rank the results from least to greatest based on the criteria provided.

Monitor regularly: Alternately, you may want to do a daily search to determine the stocks that will experience the

the greatest range of movement in the coming hours. To do so, you will want to create a new list of stocks every evening to ensure that you will be ready to go when the market opens. This list can then be made up of stocks that have shown higher volatility in the previous day either in terms of gains or in terms of losses. Adding in volume to these criteria will then help to make sure the results will likely continue to generate the kind of volume that day trading successfully requires. Useful filters for this search include an average volume that is greater than one million and the more you increase the minimum volume the fewer results you'll see.

When using this strategy, it is especially important to pick out any stocks that are likely to see major news releases before the next day as these are almost guaranteed to make the price move in several random directions before ultimately settling down. As such, it is often best to wait until after the details of the release are known and you can more accurately determine what the response is, though not so long that you miss out on the combination of high volume and high volatility. If you don't already have an earnings calendar bookmarked, the one available for free from Yahoo Finance! Is well respected.

Monitor intraday volatility: Another option that is worth considering is doing your research during the day as a means of determining which stocks are experiencing the greatest overall amount of movement at the moment.

Chapter 7

Common Day Trading Mistakes to Avoid

A side from doing the right things, you'll also need to refrain from certain things to succeed as a day trader. Here are some of the most common day trading mistakes you should avoid committing.

Excessive Day Trading

By excessive, I mean executing too many day trades. One of the most common mistakes many newbie day traders make is assuming that they can become day trading ninjas in just a couple of weeks if they trade often enough to get it right. But while more practice can eventually translate into day trading mastery, later on, it doesn't mean you can cram all that practice in a very short period of time via very frequent day trading. The adage "the more, the merrier" doesn't necessarily apply to day trading.

Remember, timing is crucial for day trading success. And timing is dependent on how the market is doing during the day. There will be days when day trading opportunities are few and far between and there'll be days when day trading opportunities abound. Don't force trades for the sake of getting enough day trades under your belt.

Even in the midst of a plethora of profitable day trading opportunities, the more the merrier still doesn't apply. Why? If you're a newbie trader, your best bet at becoming a day trading ninja at the soonest possible time is to concentrate on one- or two-day trades per day only. By limiting your day trades, to just one or two, you have the opportunity to closely monitor and learn from your trades.

Can you imagine executing 5 or more trades daily as a newbie and monitor all those positions simultaneously? You'll only get confused and overwhelmed and worse, you may even miss day trading triggers and signals and fail to profitably close your positions.

Winging It

If you want to succeed as a day trader, you need to hold each trading day in reverence and high esteem. How do you do that? By planning your day trading strategies for the day and executing those strategies instead of just winging them.

As cliché as it may sound, failing to plan is planning to fail. And considering the financial stakes involved in day trading, you shouldn't go through your trading days without any plan on hand. Luck favors those who are prepared and planning can convince lady luck that you are prepared.

Expecting Too Much Too Soon

This much is true about day trading: it's one of the most exciting and exhilarating jobs in the world! And stories many day traders tell of riches accumulated through this economic activity add more excitement, desire, and urgency for many to get into it.

However, too much excitement and desire resulting from many day trading success stories can be very detrimental to newbie day traders. Let me correct myself: it is detrimental to newbie day traders. Why?

Such stories, many of which are probably urban legends, give newbies unrealistic expectations of quick and easy day trading riches. Many beginner day traders get the impression that day trading is a get-rich-quick scheme!

It's not. What many day traders hardly brag about are the times they also lost money and how long it took them to master the craft enough to quit their jobs and do it full time. And even rarer are stories of the myriad number of people who's attempted day trading and failed? It's the dearth of such stories that tend to make day trading neophytes have unrealistic expectations about day trading.

What's the problem with lofty day trading expectations? Here's the problem: if you have very unrealistic expectations, it's almost certain that you'll fail. It's because unrealistic expectations can't be met and therefore, there are zero chances for success.

One of the most unrealistic expectations surrounding day trading is being able to double one's initial trading capital in a couple of months, at most. Similar to such expectations is that of being able to quit one's day job and live an abundant life in just a few months via day trading. Successful day traders went through numerous failures, too, before they succeeded at day trading and were able to do it for a living.

If you decide to give day trading a shot, have realistic expectations. Don't even expect to profit soon. Instead take the initial losses as they come, limiting them through sensible stop-loss limits, and learning from them. Eventually, you'll get the hang of it and your day trading profits will start eclipsing your day trading losses.

Changing Strategies Frequently

Do you know how to ride a bike? If not, do you know someone who does? Whether it's you or somebody you know, learning how to ride a bike wasn't instant. It took time and a couple of falls and bruises along the way.

But despite falls, scratches, and bruises, you or that person you know stuck to learning how to ride a bike and with enough time and practice, succeeded in doing so. It was because you or the other person knew that initial failures mean that riding a bike was impossible. It's just challenging at first.

It's the same with learning how to day trade profitably. You'll need to give yourself enough time and practice to master it. Just because you suffered trading losses, in the beginning, doesn't mean it's not working or it's not for you. It probably means you haven't mastered it yet. But if you quit and shift to a new trading strategy or plan quickly, you'll have to start again from scratch, extend your learning time, and possibly lose more money than you would've if you stuck around to your initial strategy long enough to give yourself a shot at day trading successfully or concluding with certainty that it's not working for you. If you frequently change your day trading strategies, i.e., you don't give yourself enough time to learn day trading strategies, your chances of mastering them become much lower. In which case, your chances of succeeding in day trading become much lower, too.

Not Analyzing Past Trades

Those who don't learn history are doomed to repeat it said writer and philosopher George Santayana. We can paraphrase it to apply to day traders, too: Those who don't learn from their day trading mistakes will be doomed to repeat them.

If you don't keep a day trading journal containing records of all your trades and more importantly, analyze them, you'll be doomed to repeat your losing day trades. It's because by not doing so, you won't be able to determine what you're doing wrong and what you should be doing instead to have more profitable day trades than losing ones.

As another saying goes: if you always do what you always did, you'll always get what you always got. Unless you analyze your past day trades regularly, you'll be doomed to repeating the same mistakes and continue losing money on them.

Ditching Correlations

We can define correlations as a relationship where one thing influences the outcome or behavior of another. A positive correlation means that both tend to move in the same direction or exhibit similar behaviors, i.e., when one goes up, the other goes up, too, and the other way around.

Correlations abound in the stock market. For example, returns on the stock market are usually negatively correlated with the Federal Reserve's interest rates, i.e., when the Feds increase interest rates, returns on stock market investments go down and vice versa.

Correlations exist across industries in the stock market, too. For example, property development stocks are positively correlated to steel and cement manufacturing stocks. This is because when the property development's booming, it buys more steel and cement from manufacturing companies, which in turn also increases their income.

Ignoring correlations during day trading increases your risks for erroneous position-taking and exiting. You may take a short position on a steel manufacturer's stock while taking a long position on a property development company's stock and if they have a positive correlation, one of those two positions will most likely end up in a loss.

But caution must be exercised with using correlations in your day trades. Don't establish correlations where there's none. Your job is to simply identify if there are observable correlations, what those correlations are, and how strong they are.

Being Greedy

Remember the story of the goose that lays golden eggs? Because the goose's owner was so greedy and couldn't wait for the goose to lay more eggs immediately, he killed the goose and cut it open.

Sadly, for the owner, there were no golden eggs inside the goose because it only created and laid one golden egg every day. His greed caused him to destroy his only wealth-generating asset.

When it comes to day trading, greed can have the same negative financial impact. Greed can make a day trader hold on to an already profitable position longer than needed and result in smaller profits later on or worse, trading losses.

If you remember my story, that was greed in action. Had I been content with the very good returns I already had and closed my position, my paper gains could've become actual gains. I let my greed control my trading and chose to hold on to that stock much longer than I needed to. That trade turned into a losing one eventually.

That's why you must be disciplined enough to stick to your day trading stop-loss and profit-taking limits. And that's why you should program those limits on your platform, too. Doing so minimizes the risks of greed hijacking your otherwise profitable day trades.

Chapter 8

Portfolio Diversification

D ay traders generally execute trades in the course of a single trading day while investors buy and hold stocks for days, weeks, months, and sometimes even a couple of years. In between these two extremes are other forms of trading. These include swing trading and position trading, among others.

Swing trading is where a trader buys an interest in a commodity or stock and holds the position for a couple of days before disposing of it. Position trading, on the other hand, is where a trader buys a stake in a commodity or stock for several weeks or even several months. While all these trades carry a certain element of risk, day trading carries the biggest risk.

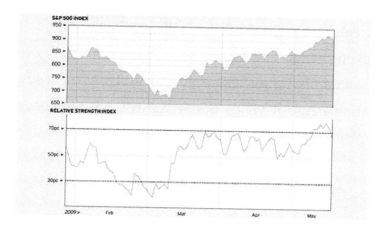

A trader with the necessary skills and access to all the important resources is bound to succeed and will encounter a steep learning curve. Professional day traders work full time, whether working for themselves or large institutions. They often set a schedule which they always adhere to. It is never wise to be a part-time day trader, a hobby trader, or a gambler. To succeed, you have to trade on a full-time basis and be as disciplined as possible.

Introduction to Diversification

Diversification is considered an effective risk management technique. It is widely used by both traders and investors. The gist behind this approach is that investing funds in just single security is extremely risky as the entire trade could potentially go up in smoke or incur significant losses.

An ideal portfolio of securities is expected to fetch a much higher return compared to a no-diversified portfolio. This is true even when compared to the returns of lower-risk investments like bonds. Generally, diversification is advisable not only because it yields better returns but also because it offers protection against losses.

Diversification Basics

Traders and investors put their funds in securities at the securities markets. One of the dangers of investing in the markets is that traders are likely to hold onto only one or two stocks at a time. This is risky because if a trade was to fail, then the trader could experience a catastrophe. However, with diversification, the risk is spread out so that regardless of what happens to some stocks, the trader still stands to be profitable. At the core of diversification is the challenge posed by unsystematic risks. When some stocks or investments perform better than others, these risks are neutralized. Therefore, for a perfectly balanced portfolio, a trader should ensure that they only deal with non-correlated assets. This means that the assets respond in opposite ways or differently to market forces.

The ideal portfolio should contain between 25 and 30 different securities. This is the perfect way of ensuring that the risk levels are drastically reduced and the only expected outcomes are profitability.

In summary, diversification is a popular strategy that is used by both traders and investors. It makes use of a wide variety of securities to improve yield and mitigate against inherent and potential risks.

It is advisable to invest or trade in a variety of assets and not all from one class. For instance, a properly diversified portfolio should include assets such as currencies, options, stocks, bonds, and so on. This approach will increase the chances of profitability and minimize risks and exposure. Diversification is even better if assets are acquired across geographical regions as well.

Best Diversification Approach

Diversification focuses on asset allocation. It consists of a plan that endeavors to allocate funds or assets appropriately across a variety of investments. When an investor diversifies his or her portfolio, then there is some level of risk that has to be accepted. However, it is also advisable to devise an exit strategy so that the investor can let go of the asset and recoup their funds. This becomes necessary when a specific asset class is not yielding any worthwhile returns compared to others.

If an investor can create an aptly diversified portfolio, their investment will be adequately covered. An adequately diversified portfolio also allows room for growth. Appropriate asset allocation is highly recommended as it allows investors a chance to leverage risk and manage any possible portfolio volatility because different assets have varying reactions to adverse market conditions.

Investor opinions on diversifications

Different investors have varying opinions regarding the type of investment scenarios they consider being ideal. Numerous investors believe that a properly diversified portfolio will likely bring in a double-digit return despite prevailing market conditions. They also agree that in the worst-case situation will be simply a general decrease in the value of the different assets. Yet with all this information out there, very few investors can achieve portfolio diversification.

So why are investors unable to simply diversify their portfolios appropriately? The answers are varied and diverse. The challenges encountered by investors in diversification include weighting imbalance, hidden correlation, underlying devaluation, and false returns, among others. While these challenges sound rather technical, they can easily be solved. The solution is also rather simple. By hacking these challenges, an investor will then be able to benefit from an aptly diversified platform.

The Process of Asset Class Allocation

There are different ways of allocating investments to assets. According to studies, most investors, including professional investors, portfolio managers, and seasoned traders rarely beat the indexes within their preferred asset class. It is also important to note that there is a visible correlation between the performance of an underlying asset class and the returns that an investor receives. In general, professional investors tend to perform more or less the same as an index within the same class asset.

Investment returns from a diversified portfolio can generally be expected to closely imitate the related asset class. Therefore, asset class choice is considered an extremely crucial aspect of an investment. It is the single more crucial aspect for the success of a particular asset class. Other factors, such as individual asset selection and market timing, only contribute about 6% of the variance in investment outcomes.

Wide Diversifications between Various Asset Classes

Diversification to numerous investors simply implies spreading their funds through a wide variety of stocks in different sectors such as health care, financial, energy, as well as medium caps, small, and large-cap companies. This is the opinion of your average investor. However, a closer look at this approach reveals that investors are simply putting their money in different sectors of the stocks class. These asset classes can very easily fall and rise when the markets do.

A reliably diversified portfolio is one where the investor or even the manager is watchful and alert because of the hidden correlation that exists between different asset classes. This correlation can easily change with time, and there are several reasons for this. One reason is international markets. Many investors often choose to diversify their portfolios with international stocks.

However, there is also a noticeable correlation across the different global financial markets. This correlation is visible not just across European markets but also emerging markets from around the world. There is also a clear correlation between equities and fixed income markets, which are generally the hallmarks of diversification.

This correlation is a challenge and is probably a result of the relationship between structured financing and investment banking. Another factor that contributes to this correlation is the rapid growth and popularity of hedge funds. Take the case where a large international organization such as a hedge fund suffers losses in a particular asset class.

Should this happen, then the firm may have to dispose of some assets across the different asset classes. This will have a multiplier effect as numerous other investments, and other investors will, therefore, be affected even though they had diversified their portfolios appropriately. This is a challenge that affects numerous investors who are probably unaware of its existence. They are also probably unaware of how it should be rectified or avoided.

Realignment of Asset Classes

One of the best approaches to solving the correlation challenge is to focus on class realignment. Asset allocation should not be considered as a static process. Asset class imbalance is a phenomenon that occurs when the securities markets develop, and different asset classes exhibit varied performance.

After a while, investors should assess their investments then diversify out of underperforming assets and instead shift this investment to other asset classes that are performing well and are profitable in the long term. Even then, it is advisable to be vigilant so that no one single asset class is overweighed as other standard risks are still inherent. Also, a prolonged bullish market can result in overweighting one of the different asset classes which could be ready for a correction. There are a couple of approaches that an investor can focus on, and these are discussed below.

Diversification and the Relative Value

Investors sometimes find asset returns to be misleading, including veteran investors. As such, it is advisable to interpret asset returns concerning the specific asset class performance. The interpretation should also take into consideration the risks that this asset class is exposed to and even the underlying currency.

When diversifying investments, it is important to think about diversifying into asset classes that come with different risk profiles. These should also be held in a variety of currencies. You should not expect to enjoy the same outcomes when investing in government bonds and technology stocks. However, it is recommended to endeavor to understand how each suits the larger investment objective.

Using such an approach, it will be possible to benefit more from a small gain from an asset within a market where the currency is increasing in value. This is as compared to a large gain from an asset within a market where the currency is in decline. As such, huge gains can translate into losses when the gains are reverted to the stronger currency. This is the reason why it is advisable to ensure that proper research and evaluation of different asset classes are conducted.

Currencies should be considered

Currency considerations are crucial when selecting asset classes to diversify in. take the Swiss franc for instance. It is one of the world's most stable currencies and has been that way since the 1940s. Because of this reason, this particular currency can be safely and reliably used to measure the performance of other currencies.

However, private investors sometimes take too long choosing and trading stocks. Such activities are both overwhelming and time-consuming. This is why, in such instances, it is advisable to approach this differently and focus more on the asset class. With this kind of approach, it is possible to be even more profitable. Proper asset allocation is crucial to successful investing. It enables investors to mitigate any investment risks as well as portfolio volatility. The reason is that different asset classes have different reactions to all the different market conditions.

Constructing a well-thought-out and aptly diversified portfolio, it is possible to have a stable and profitable portfolio that even outperforms the index of assets. Investors also have the opportunity to leverage against any potential risks because of different reactions by the different market conditions.

Chapter 9

Options Day Trading Rules for Success

There is more to options day trading than just having a style or a strategy. If that was all it took, then you could just adopt those that are proven to work and just stick with them. Yes, options day trading styles and strategy are important but they are not the end-all-be-all of this career.

The winning factor is the options day trader himself or herself. *You* are the factor that determines whether or not you will win or lose in this career. Only taking the time to develop your expertise, seeking guidance when necessary, and being dedicated allows a person to move from a novice options day trader to an experienced one that is successful and hitting his or her target goals.

To develop into the options day trader you want to be, being disciplined is necessary. There are options day trading rules that can help you develop that necessary discipline. You will make mistakes. Every beginner in any niche does and even experienced options day traders are human and thus, have bad days too.

Knowing common mistakes helps you avoid many of these mistakes and takes away much of the guesswork. Having rules to abide by helps you avoid these mistakes as well.

Below, I have listed 11 rules that every options day trader must know. Following them is entirely up to you but know that they are proven to help beginner options day traders turn into winning options day traders.

Rule for Success #1 – Have Realistic Expectations

It is sad to say that many people who enter the options trading industry are doing so to make a quick buck. Options trading is not a get-rich-quick scheme. It is a reputable career that has made many people rich but that is only because these people have put in the time, effort, study, and dedication to learning the craft and mastering it. Mastery does not happen overnight and beginner options day traders need to be prepared for that learning curve and to have the fortitude to stick with day trading options even when it becomes tough.

Losses are also part of the game. No trading style or strategy will guarantee gains all the time. The best options traders have a winning percentage of about 80% and a losing average of approximately 20%. That is why an options day trader needs to be a good money manager and a good risk manager. Be prepared for eventual losses and be prepared to minimize those losses.

Rule for Success #2 – Start Small to Grow a Big Portfolio

Caution is the name of the game when you just get started with day trading options. Remember that you are still learning options trading and developing an understanding of the financial market. Do not jump the gun even if you are eager. After you have practiced paper trading, start with smaller options positions and steadily grow your standing as you get a lay of the options day trading land. This strategy allows you to keep your losses to a minimum and to develop a systematic way of entering positions.

Rule for Success #3 – Know Your Limits

You may be tempted to trade as much as possible to develop a winning monthly average but that strategy will have the opposite effect and land you with a losing average. Remember that every options trader needs careful consideration before that contract is set up. Never overtrade and tie up your investment fund.

Rule for Success #4 – Be Mentally, Physically and Emotionally Prepared Every Day

This is a mentally, physically, and emotionally tasking career and you need to be able to meet the demands of this career. That means keeping your body, mind, and heart in good health at all times. Ensure that you schedule time for self-care every day. That can be as simple as taking the time to read for recreation to having an elaborate self-care routine carved out in the evenings.

Not keeping your mind, heart, and head in optimum health means that they are more likely to fail you. Signs that you need to buckle up and care for yourself more diligently include being constantly tired, being short-tempered, feeling preoccupied, and being easily distracted.

To ensure you perform your best every day, here a few tasks that you need to perform:

- Get the recommended amount of sleep daily. This is between 7 and 9 hours for an adult.
- Practice a balanced diet. The brain and body need adequate nutrition to work their best. Include

fruits, complex carbs, and veggies in this diet and reduce the consumption of processed foods.

- Eat breakfast lunch and dinner every day. Fuel your mind and body with the main meals. Eating a healthy breakfast is especially important because it helps set the tone for the rest of the day.
- Exercise regularly. Being inactive increases your risk of developing chronic diseases like heart disease, certain cancers, and other terrible health consequences. Adding just a few minutes of exercise to your daily routine not only reduces those risks but also allows your brain to function better, which is a huge advantage for an options day trader.
- Drink alcohol in moderation or not at all.
- Stop smoking.
- Reduce stress contributors in your environment.

Rule for Success #5 – Do Your Homework Daily

Get up early and study the financial environment before the market opens and look at the news. This allows you to develop a daily options trading plan. The process of analyzing the financial climate before the market opens is called pre-market preparation. It is a necessary task that needs to be performed every day to asset competition and to align your overall strategy with the short-term conditions of that day.

An easy way to do this is to develop a pre-market checklist. An example of a pre-market checklist includes but is not limited to:

- Checking the individual markets that you frequently trade options in or plan to trade options in to evaluate support and resistance.
- Checking the news to assess whether events that could affect the market developed overnight.
- Assessing what other options traders are doing to determined volume and competition.
- Determining what safe exits for losing positions are.
- Considering the seasonality of certain markets are some as affected by the day of the week, the month of the year, *etc.*

Rule for Success #6 – Analyze Your Daily Performance

To determine if the options day trading style and strategies that you have adopted are working for you, you need to track your performance. At the most basic, this needs to be done on a daily basis because you are trading options

daily. This will allow you to notice patterns in your profit and loss. This can lead to you determining the why and how of these gains and losses. These determinations lead to fine-tuning your daily processes for maximum returns. These daily performance reviews allow you to also make determinations on the long-term activity of your options day trading career.

Rule for Success #7 – Do Not Be Greedy

If you are fortunate enough to make a 100% return on your investment, do not be greedy and try to reap more benefits from the position. You might have the position turn on you and you can lose everything. When and if such a rare circumstance happens to you, sell your position and take the profits.

Rule for Success #8 – Pay Attention to Volatility

Volatility speaks to how likely a price change will occur over a specific amount of time on the financial market. Volatility can work for an options day trader or against the options day trader. It all depends on what the options day trader is trying to accomplish and what his or her current position is.

Many external factors affect volatility and such factors include the economic climate, global events, and news reports. Strangles and straddles strategies are great for use in volatile markets.

There are different types of volatility and they include:

- Price volatility, which describes how the price of an asset increases or decreases based on the supply and demand of that asset.
- Historical volatility, which is a measure of how an asset has performed over the last 12 months.
- Implied volatility, which is a measure of how an asset will perform in the future.

Rule for Success #9 – Use the Greeks

Greeks are a collection of measures that provide a gauge of an option's price sensitivity concerning other factors. Each Greek is represented by a letter from the Greek alphabet. These Greeks use complex formulas to be determined but they are the system that option pricing is based on. Even though these calculations can be complex, they can be done quickly and efficiently so that options day traders can use them as a method of advancing their trades for the most profitable position.

Chapter 10

Trading With the Trend

Buying Calls

So let's get started by considering the most basic strategy of all, and that is buying a call option because you believe that the price of the stock is going to increase soon. Therefore, the goal was buying a call option would be to purchase it at the right moment and then hope that the stock will go up so much that we can sell the option for a profit. This all sounds simple enough almost like something that you could never miss. Unfortunately, in practice, it's a lot more challenging than it sounds on paper. The first consideration is going to be whether or not you purchase an option that is in the money or out of the money. If this strategy works maybe that is not an important consideration provided that it's not too far out of the money.

The reason that people decide to purchase out-of-the-money options is that they are cheaper as compared to in-the-money options. It's also a fact that if the stock is moving in the right direction out of the money options will gain at price as well.

So, if someone tells you that you can't make profits from out-of-the-money options they are not being completely honest with you. You can make profits but it's always going to depend on how the stock is moving and the distance between your strike price and the share price.

The best strategy to use when going with out-of-the-money options is to purchase them slightly out of the money by a dollar or two. What this does is ensures the price of the option is going to be significantly impacted by changes in the stock price. Second, you wouldn't be purchasing a call unless there was a good chance that the share price would be moving up. So, if you are close in price to the market price, and there is a reasonable amount of time until expiration, there would be a good chance that the share price would rise above your strike price. If that happens it could mean significant profits for you. Of course, you can always take the risk of putting it a little bit more money upfront and investing in a call option that is already in the money. If the stock price rises, that is only going to solidify your position. You also have a little bit of insurance there. That comes from the fact that if you choose a decent strike price there is a solid chance it will stay in the money and so even if it doesn't gain much value you will be able to sell it and either not lose that much, or still make a profit.

So, what are we hoping for with this strategy? The main hope would be that there is a large trend that takes off so that we can write the trend and earn a healthy profit. Since options are so sensitive to the price of the stock if such a trend occurs it's pretty easy to make decent money. The key, of course, is getting in the trend at the right time and knowing when to get out of the position.

Market Awareness

The first thing to keep in mind is what I call market awareness. This involves being aware of everything that could impact the price of the underlying stock. This can mean not only paying attention to the chart of the stock, but you also need to be paying attention to the news and not just financial news. So, let's take a recent example by looking at Facebook. In recent months Facebook has been constantly in the news. Some of the news has been good such as a decent earnings report. On the other hand, Facebook has been receiving some pushback from governments around the world. One of the issues that have been raised is privacy concerns. Facebook is also catching a lot of flak over its plan to create a cryptocurrency. So here is the point. Every time one of these news items comes out, it's a potential for a trend. But there are a couple of problems with this. In many cases, you simply don't know when dramatic news is going to come out. So, you have to be paying attention at all times and have your money ready to go. The best-case scenario is purchasing an option for the day before some large event. People are often reacting strongly in the markets when there is a good or bad jobs report or the GDP number is about to come out. So what you would want to do in that case is first of all pay attention to the news and see what the expectations are of all the market watchers that everyone pays attention to. Of course, they are often off the mark but it gives you some kind of idea of where things might be heading. If a good jobs report is expected, then you might want to invest in an index fund such as DIA which is for the Dow Jones industrial average. One thing you know is that a good jobs report is going to send the Dow and the S&P 500 up by large amounts. So, the key is to be prepared by purchasing your options the day before. But on the other hand, you might be wrong with your guess, which could be costly.

You could wait until the news comes out. But I have to say from my experience trading this is a difficult
proposition. The reason is you would be surprised how quickly the price rises when dramatic news comes out either way. So, when one sense is a safer way to approach things but the price

might be rising so fast that you find it nearly impossible to purchase the options. That you can execute a trade the trend might even be over. But if you're there in the middle of the action you might as well try and then you can ride it out and probably make pretty good profits.

Some people like to sit around and study stock market charts. During everyday trading when there hasn't been any dramatic news announcement or something like that which will massively impact the price of the underlying stock, looking at candlesticks charts along with moving averages can give you a good idea of went to enter or exit trades. However, it's fair to say that there is a little bit of hype surrounding these tools. The fact is they don't always work because they are easily misled or maybe it's the human mind that is misled by short-term changes that go against the main trend but are temporary. So, you can make the mistake while following candlesticks and moving averages of seeing evidence of the sudden downtrend and then selling your position, only to find out that the downtrend wasn't real and it was only a temporary setback soon followed by a resumption of the main trend. So that is something to be careful about.

Setting Profit Goals

If you were going to trade this way probably the best thing to do is to set a specific level of modest profit to use as a goal. One that I use is a $50 per options contract. Some people may be more conservative so you could set a goal of $30 profit. Some people might be more risk-oriented. I would honestly discourage that kind of thinking because sitting there hoping for $100 profit per contract, while it is possible, you may also find yourself in a situation more often than not where you lose money. What might happen is you have to sit around waiting too long to hit that magic number and it never materializes. Options can quickly turn from winners into losers because they magnify the changes in the underlying stock price by 100. So, it's very easy to lose money quickly.

In my experience, the $50 price level is pretty good. The only time that this value has hurt me is when I see the $50 profit hit and I failed to sell my positions because I got greedy watching the upward trend and hoped for even more money. So that is something you should avoid it's better to stick to your law, whatever you happen to pick, and then always implemented no matter what the situation is. Remember that there is always another day to trade. You're trading career never depends on a single trade or a single day's trading. The bottom line is that it's better to take a small profit her option contract and per trade and then go back and trade some more, then it is to hope for large profits that may never materialize. Also, you can always magnify small profits by trading multiple options at once. So, if you trade 10 options and you're only going to accept a $30 profit on the trade, which means in total you could make $300. It doesn't matter what specific number you pick, but you should pick a value and stick to it. If I have a regret from trading the only regret is that I didn't stick to the rules that I have set for myself.

Day Trading?

For those who are not aware, if you are labeled a patterned day trader, you need to have $25,000 in your account, and you need to open a margin account. So, for most individual traders with small accounts, the last thing you want is to be labeled as a day trader. However, since options lose a lot of value from time decay, and many trends are short-lived, you may find yourself in situations where you have to enter a day trade. But if you are doing this make sure that you only do three per five-day trading period. That way you will avoid getting the designation and all the problems that might come about with it. In this case, if you buy a lot of several options that have the same strike price and the same expiration date, those are going to count as the same security. That may result in problems if you need to unload them all on the same day. One way to get around this is to purchase call options with slightly different strike prices instead of getting a bunch with all the same strike prices. Of course, if you were going to hold your positions overnight and risk the loss from time decay having to do that may not be something to worry about.

Trading Puts

Trading puts using these techniques is going to be the same, with the only difference being that you would be looking for downward trends. This is a little bit different because people are accustomed to thinking in terms of rising stock prices means profits. So, it might be hard to wrap your mind around the idea of profiting from stock market declines.

Conclusion

Thank you for making it through to the end of *Day Trading Strategies*, let's hope it was informative and able to provide you with all of the tools and information you need to manage your journey in the market trade.

Day trading is described as the process of speculation of risks and either buying or selling financial instruments on the same day of trading. The financial instruments are bought at a lower price and later sold at a higher price. People who participate in this form of trade are mostly referred to as speculators. Day trading is a different form of trading known as swing trading. Swing trading involves selling financial instruments and latter buying them at a lower price. It is a form of trade that has several people have invested their time and capital in. The potential for making profits is very high. However, it is also accompanied by the high potential of making huge percentages of loss. People who are terms as high-risk takers have the potential to realize good amounts of profits or huge losses. It is because of the nature of the trade. The losses are experienced because of several variables that are always present in trading. The gains and individual experiences are brought to light by margin buying.

There is a big difference between swing trade and day trade. The difference hails from their definitions, it goes a mile ahead to time spent in and risks involved in both forms of trade. Day trade has lower risk involvement but one has to spend more of his or her time, unlike swing trade. Day traders are prone to participating in two forms of trade which are long trades or short trades. Long trade involves an individual purchasing the financial instruments and selling them after them increasing in value. On the other hand, short trade involves selling financial instruments and later purchasing them after their prices have dropped.

The trading market has undergone through several advancements. The major change was witnessed during the deregulation process. There was the creation of electronic financial markets during this period. One of the major innovations was the high-frequency trading index. It uses heavy algorithms to enable huge financial firms in stock trading to perform numerous orders in seconds. It is advantageous because it can also predict market trends.

The process of day trading has several challenges. An individual is supposed to be able to make a good decision during two important moments. The first moment is during a good streak and the other is during moments an individual has a poor run. At this point risk management and trading, psychology comes in handy to help an individual in the trade.

One is not supposed to panic or make hasty decisions during these moments. An individual need to have an effective watchlist. A good watchlist built by a trader is supposed to be able to understand the modern trading markets. This is made possible when it features stocks in play, float and market capital, pre-market grippers, real-time intraday scans, and planning trade based on scanners. The success of day trading is also incumbent on effective strategies. The common strategies include ABCD patterns, bag flag momentum, reversal trading, movie average trading, and opening range breakouts.

There are also advanced strategies that can be used to ensure the success of day trading. Three of these strategies are one stock in play, bull flag, and a fallen angel. With the use of these strategies, a successful trader builds his or her trading business step by step. The common steps involve building a watchlist, having a trading plan, and knowing how to execute.